Telephones

household history

17F11

Telephones

Elaine Marie Alphin

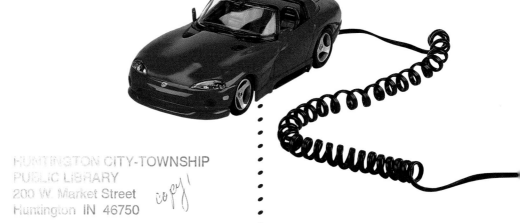

‰ Carolrhoda Books, Inc./Minneapolis

The photographs in this book are reproduced through the courtesy of: © Hulton Deutsch Collection/Corbis, pp. 1, 35 (left); © Jim Simondet/Patty Ruben Miller/Independent Picture Service, pp. 2, 3, 5, 6, 7 (right), 11, 13, 31, 34 (left, right), 39 (both), 41 (left); © Ron Watts/Corbis, p. 7 (left); © Moshe Shai/Corbis, p. 12; © Dallas and John Heaton/Corbis, p. 14; © Stock Montage, p. 15 (left); © Bettmann/Corbis, pp. 15 (right), 16, 17, 19 (both), 23; © Library of Congress, pp. 18 (right), (LC-USZ62-29978-2188), 27 (bottom), (LC-MSS-51268-6); © Corbis, p. 18 (left); Western Union, p. 21; Brown Brothers, p. 22; From: *Phillip Reis: Inventor of the Telephone,* p. 24; Smithsonian Institution, E & MP Collections, (negative # 45770), p. 25; From: *Alexander Graham Bell: The Life and Times of the Man Who Invented the Telephone,* p. 26; Property of AT&T Archives. Reprinted with permission of AT&T, pp. 27 (top), 28, 29; © Archive Photos, pp. 30, 33 (left), 36 (both); © Hirz/Archive Photos, p. 32; © American Stock/Archive Photos, p. 33 (right); © Tom Neiman/Stock Montage, p. 34 (middle); © Lawrence Manning/Corbis, p. 35 (right); RadioShack Corporation, p. 38; Minnesota Historical Society, p. 40; © Robert Maass/Corbis, p. 41 (right); Tate Gallery, London/Art Resource, NY, p. 42; Hollywood Book & Poster, p. 43; © AFP/Corbis, p. 44.

Front cover photographs appear courtesy of: © Jim Simondet/Patty Ruben Miller/Independent Picture Service, top left, top right, middle left; © Dave Nagel/Stone, bottom right; Property of AT&T Archives. Reprinted with permission of AT&T, bottom left.

For Art, who has filled our home with teddy bear and Snoopy telephones

Words that appear in **bold** in the text are listed in the glossary on page 46.

Text copyright © 2001 by Elaine Marie Alphin
Illustrations on pp. 8–10, 44–45 by Tim Seeley, © 2001 by Carolrhoda Books, Inc.

Carolrhoda Books, Inc.
A division of Lerner Publishing Group
241 First Avenue North
Minneapolis, MN 55401 U.S.A.

Website address: www.lernerbooks.com

Library of Congress Cataloging-in-Publication Data

Alphin, Elaine Marie.
  Telephones / Elaine Marie Alphin.
    p. cm — (Household history)
  Includes index.
  Summary: Presents the technological development of the telephone through a description of the various inventions that led up to it, then examines the role of the phone in popular culture.
    ISBN 1-57505-432-9 (lib. bdg. : alk. paper)
    1. Telephone—Juvenile literature. [1. Telephone.] I. Title. II. Series.
TK6165.A58 2001
621.385—dc21   99-050528

Manufactured in the United States of America
1 2 3 4 5 6 – JR – 06 05 04 03 02 01

Contents

Is Anybody There?

"Help!"

You hear a shout and look out your front window. A car just ran into a bicycle in the street, and the kid on the ground isn't moving. Your parents aren't home. You can't help—or can you?

You grab your telephone and dial 911. Almost immediately an operator asks, "What is the nature of your emergency?" You describe the accident and give the address. Within minutes an ambulance pulls up, and paramedics help the injured bike rider onto a stretcher.

What would you have done without a telephone? If you had needed to run all the way to the nearest hospital for help, how long would it have taken you?

A telephone is often the fastest way to reach help in a pinch.

Kids usually have no trouble finding reasons to use the telephone.

Telephones come in handy even when there's no emergency. You can call a friend to check on homework or make plans for a movie. Calling your grandparents is a good way to make sure they get you that video game you want for your birthday, instead of socks and underwear. On average, kids talk on the phone for about half an hour every day. The average American household has three telephones to handle the traffic!

You could always talk to your friend at school or write your grandparents a letter. But a telephone is really important when you have to reach someone quickly. It may seem like magic when you pick up the receiver, punch in a number, and hear a voice from miles away. But it's magic made from electricity and sound.

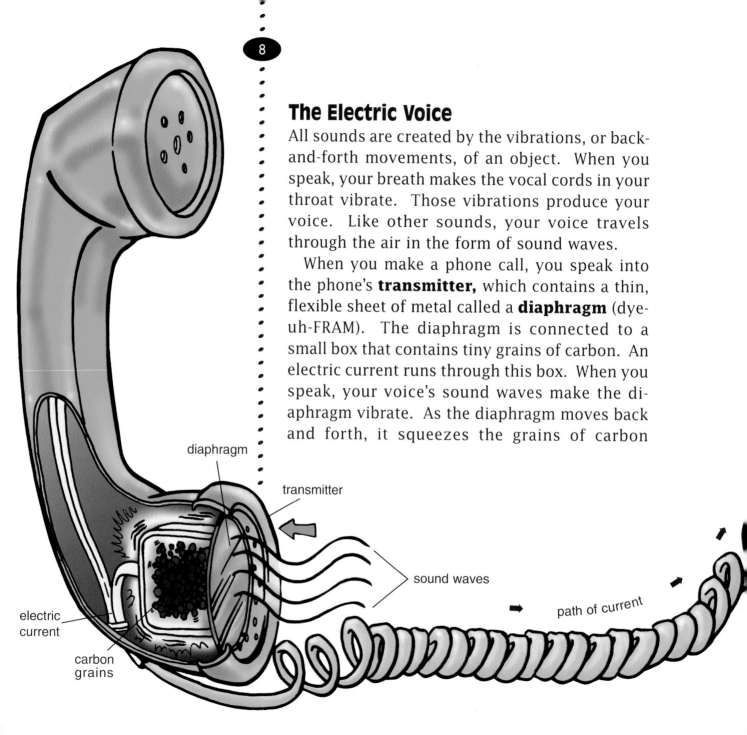

The Electric Voice

All sounds are created by the vibrations, or back-and-forth movements, of an object. When you speak, your breath makes the vocal cords in your throat vibrate. Those vibrations produce your voice. Like other sounds, your voice travels through the air in the form of sound waves.

When you make a phone call, you speak into the phone's **transmitter,** which contains a thin, flexible sheet of metal called a **diaphragm** (dye-uh-FRAM). The diaphragm is connected to a small box that contains tiny grains of carbon. An electric current runs through this box. When you speak, your voice's sound waves make the diaphragm vibrate. As the diaphragm moves back and forth, it squeezes the grains of carbon

diaphragm

transmitter

sound waves

electric current

carbon grains

path of current

receiver

electromagnet

sound waves

together, then allows them to scatter. When the grains are squeezed together, the electric current grows stronger. When the grains are scattered, the current grows weaker. The result is a varying electric current that carries your voice. This current is called an **analog signal.**

The analog signal travels through a wire to the **receiver** of the phone you're calling. Inside the receiver, the wire is coiled around a piece of metal. The current magnetizes the metal, creating an **electromagnet.** The electromagnet attracts a diaphragm in the receiver. Because the current's strength varies, the strength of the electromagnet varies, too. As the electromagnet gets stronger and weaker, it makes the metal diaphragm vibrate, just like the diaphragm in your transmitter. When your friend holds the receiver to her ear, she'll hear sound waves that sound almost exactly like your voice!

diaphragm

analog signal

From One Phone to Another

Your telephone line runs into either an overhead cable on a pole, or an underground cable. That cable leads to a central **switching station,** where it meets many cables from other areas. When you push the buttons on your telephone to dial a friend's number, each button sends an electric signal out to the switching station. There, a tone decoder recognizes the digit from its musical tone.

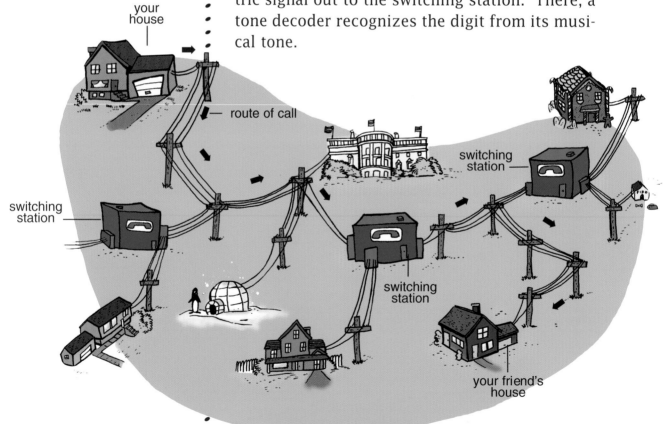

your house

route of call

switching station

switching station

switching station

your friend's house

Telephones used to have dials, not buttons. When you dialed the number 3, three clicks traveled along the wire to the switching station. The computer counted the clicks for each number you dialed, then routed your call to the correct phone number. It took about eleven seconds to complete a seven-digit call. In the late 1960s, engineers developed buttons that signaled the computer by a musical tone, shortening the dialing time to under eight seconds. Since then, dialing has become even faster.

Based on the digits you dial, a master computer opens a series of switches for the electric current carrying your call. These switches are called **relays.** Relays route your call from one switching station to another, until they reach the local station that can link your call to the line that leads to your friend's house. If you live in Virginia and you call your grandparents in Oregon, you'll dial ten digits instead of seven. Those extra three digits, the area code, tell the master computer in the switching station to find a route to a different part of the country.

Before your friend picks up the phone, it has to ring. Electricity travels into your friend's phone to sound a tone or ring a bell. You hear a ringing sound at your end, but that isn't actually your friend's phone. It's a tone called a **ringback** that lets you know your call has gone through.

Perhaps you use a cordless phone when you're lying out by the pool. Or your parents might have a cellular phone in their car. These telephones use **radio waves** to transmit your call. Radio waves travel through the air, not through wires.

A cellular phone comes in handy for this Bedouin camel rider.

Radio waves are also used for some types of long-distance calls. These calls can be transmitted through a satellite in outer space to the other side of the world in less than a second.

When you speak into the transmitter of a cordless or cellular phone, your voice is changed into an electric current as usual, but that current is then transformed into radio waves. The radio waves travel from your phone's antenna to a radio tower. The tower sends your signal to a mobile switching office, which transforms the radio signal back to an electric current and routes it to a central switching station.

All these different telephones need electricity to work. So how did people talk to each other across long distances before electric power was harnessed?

Cellular phones are portable and convenient —but they also cost more to use than traditional phones.

Sending
a Message

The Appian Way, part of an ancient Roman system of roads, helped messengers race from Rome to the Adriatic Sea.

The world's first marathon runner wasn't running to stay in shape. He was making the equivalent of a long-distance phone call. In 490 B.C., the Greeks defeated the Persians at Marathon. Greek tradition describes how a long-distance runner named Pheidippides carried the news twenty-five miles to Athens.

But people wanted to communicate faster than messengers could run. The Greeks used carrier pigeons in 450 B.C. to get their messages from one place to another more quickly. By 350 B.C., a system of lighthouses helped the Greeks

The ancient Greeks communicated with smoke signals that stood for letters of the Greek alphabet.

communicate from Athens to Persia. These lighthouses had mirrors that could reflect light from one tower to the next. In Africa, signal drums could carry messages over long distances. European armies used drums and bugles to signal their soldiers. Native Americans communicated with smoke signals on the plains and in the Southwest through the 1800s.

Signal fires alone sometimes carried messages. In 1588 the English were expecting the Spanish Armada to attack. They laid bonfires all over England, one in sight of the next. As the Spanish ships came into view, the English lit the first bonfire. At the sight of that fire, the next one was lit. In only a few hours, the news spread across England, and citizens armed themselves to fight. Like the early Greek lighthouses, signal fires were an effective way to transmit a simple message—but what if you needed to ask a question?

An 1886 engraving shows how Native Americans used smoke signals in the Southwest.

Not Quite a Telephone

In England, Robert Hooke puzzled over this problem. In 1664 he invented a simple wire communication device. The sound waves of a speaker's voice made the wire vibrate, transmitting the sounds along the wire. Hooke claimed his device could carry sound quite a long way in an instant. It even worked when the wire was bent at angles. If you wanted to talk to ten friends at different times, however, you would need ten wires, one going to each friend's house. A town could get pretty tangled in all those wires!

Despite the inconvenience of this wire device, people wanted to talk to each other. In fact, the word *telephone* had already been invented—there just wasn't an invention to fit it yet! In 1780 people called a megaphone a telephone, even though it only magnified the speaker's voice so it could reach a little farther. They also referred to a speaking tube as a telephone. A speaking tube connected the bridge of a ship to the captain's quarters, or the main room of a house to the kitchen or servant's quarters.

Like Hooke's wire device, however, a speaking tube carried the voice only along a single connection. If a house

An ancient leader shouts through what may have been the world's first megaphone more than 2,800 years ago.

Binoculars allow people to see flag signals over very long distances, as shown by this shipboard semaphore team of the mid-1900s.

owner wanted to speak to both the kitchen and the servant's quarters, she had to have two separate speaking tubes.

In 1792 French engineer Claude Chappe invented a system called semaphore that could carry a signal over long distances. Chappe built tall towers within sight of each other. Each tower had a post with movable flags. By moving the flags into different positions for each letter, a person could spell out messages that could be transmitted from tower to tower. Chappe called his system an "optical telegraph," but it was a long way from a true telegraph—a machine that could send instant messages.

A message sent by semaphore could travel 100 miles, from Paris to Lille, in just over two minutes. Paris could receive a message from Calais, nearly 180 miles away, in four minutes!

Samuel Morse

*Hans Christian Oersted
(left)*

Wires across the World

The next big break for communication didn't come until the 1830s, and it took the combined efforts of science and art. American Samuel Morse was studying painting in Europe. As interested as he was in art, he found himself even more fascinated with Chappe's semaphore. Morse thought it was much better than the mail system, which could take weeks to deliver a letter. But he didn't think semaphore was fast enough.

Morse wondered if electricity could speed things up. In 1819 Danish physicist Hans Christian Oersted had observed that a compass's magnetized needle moved in reaction to a nearby wire carrying electricity. The electric current was acting as a magnet! Oersted's work was the first step in the discovery of a new science, electromagnetism.

As Morse sailed back to America in 1832, he sketched plans for an electromagnetic telegraph system with wires strung around the world. Morse experimented for years and produced a working telegraph in 1837. The sender tapped a switch that completed an electric circuit. This circuit sent a current down the wire to an electromagnet at the receiving end. The electromagnet attracted an iron bar, making a clicking sound. Morse created a code that used different clicks to represent dots and dashes, which in turn represented letters.

Samuel Morse sends the first official, public telegraph message in 1844: "What hath God wrought?"

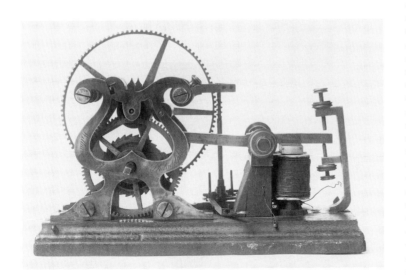

An early version of Morse's telegraph

A Dotty Code

American Morse code (below) is based on dots and dashes. Morse's telegraph had a bar that completed the current briefly for a dot and longer for a dash. At the receiving end of the telegraph, a hard-pointed rod stamped the code on a continuous roll of paper. Ships and trains all over the world used versions of Morse code to send and receive messages until the invention of fax machines and telegraphs that could print words.

A •–	J –•–•	S •••
B –•••	K –•–	T –
C •• •	L –	U ••–
D –••	M ––	V •••–
E •	N –•	W •––
F •–•	O • •	X •–••
G ––•	P •••••	Y •• ••
H ••••	Q ••–•	Z ••• •
I ••	R • ••	

Morse realized that the electric current grew weaker as it traveled over a long distance. He created a series of stations that boosted the charge on the current so it could travel farther. Telegraph lines went up across America. The Western Union Telegraph Company was founded in 1855 and soon became the leader in the field.

While Morse's telegraph could send accurate messages quickly and reliably, only one message could travel on a telegraph wire at a time. If three people in Boston wanted to send messages to Philadelphia, they had to wait. Western Union needed a way to **multiplex,** or carry more than one message on a line. Two inventors tackled the problem: Elisha Gray and Alexander Graham Bell.

In many areas, Western Union employees had to transport telegraph poles and wires by horse and cart.

Musical Telegraphs

Alexander Graham Bell was born in Scotland but had moved to America and become a teacher at the Boston School for the Deaf. Bell wanted to help people communicate better. When he heard about the problem of multiplexing telegraph lines, his interest in invention was sparked. He experimented with connecting tuning forks of different pitches to a wire. In 1872 he attached a set of reeds to the receiving end of a wire. Each reed was tuned to the exact pitch of a tuning fork, so it would sound only when that tuning fork was struck.

Bell realized that if each telegraph transmission were sent on a different pitch, then the same wire could carry many different signals at once. This **harmonic telegraph** could solve the multiplexing problem. And if a wire could carry a musical tone, could it also carry a voice?

American Elisha Gray was asking himself the same question. In 1874 Gray saw his nephew playing with some electrical equipment in the family's empty zinc-lined bathtub. The boy held the live end of a wire in one hand while rubbing the dry bottom of the tub with his other hand. Gray could hear a sound coming from beneath his nephew's hand. This sound was exactly the same pitch as the sound made by the machine that powered the electric wire! Gray had just discovered the same idea for the harmonic telegraph as Bell.

Both Gray and Bell knew the wires could carry sounds, but neither knew how to transmit voices. Meanwhile, in Germany, a schoolteacher had already invented the very first telephone.

Alexander Graham Bell (opposite page) and Elisha Gray (right) became fierce rivals in the race to improve communication.

Philipp Reis

Words across the Miles

Philipp Reis was a German physicist, inventor, and schoolteacher. His inventions never seemed to make money, but one of them proved useful in his school. Experimenting with electric current and the conversion of sound vibrations to electrical impulses, Reis designed a machine in 1860 that could conduct the sound of voices across wires. He promptly strung wires across the school campus, connecting several classrooms. His students never knew when he might be listening in on them!

Reis's *telephon* used a steel rod about the size of a knitting needle to receive sounds. A coil of wire around the steel rod transformed it into an electromagnet. As current passed through the wire, the electromagnet made the needle vibrate, generating sound waves. Reis used a diaphragm made of animal skin in his transmitter. This distorted the sounds, because the skin would loosen or tighten depending on the amount of moisture in the air. Still, Reis could hear his students, and Reis telephones were manufactured and sold. German scientists, however, dismissed his invention as a toy. Reis died in 1874, convinced that he had participated in the birth of a great invention that only future generations would appreciate. He was right.

Reis's telephon *didn't work well enough to be commonly used, but it was the first invention of its kind.*

Down to the Wire

In America Alexander Graham Bell and Elisha Gray were still working on the problem of multiplexing telegraph lines. But Gray could see the possibility of transmitting voices. He experimented by running a wire through an electricity-conducting liquid in his transmitter. The sound waves of a speaker's voice caused the wire and the liquid to vibrate, generating a current and transmitting the voice. However, Gray's lawyers told him that the real money lay in the harmonic telegraph. Not entirely convinced, Gray drew a sketch of his liquid transmitter and filed a patent caveat—a notice that he would soon file a complete patent application—on Valentine's Day, 1876.

A drawing from Elisha Gray's patent caveat

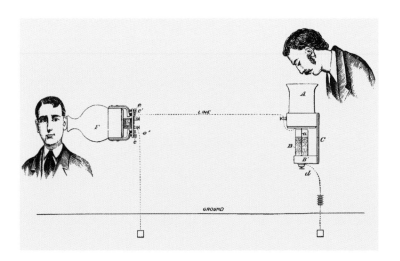

Bell's advisers told him to focus on the harmonic telegraph, too. He hired a young mechanic, Thomas A. Watson, to help. In 1875 Bell built a machine that stretched from one end of the building to the other. One day Watson plucked one of the machine's reeds to keep it vibrating. Bell heard a loud *twang* at his end and rushed to find out what had happened. In plucking the reed, Watson had generated an electrical current—and that current carried the exact sound of the vibrating reed to Bell's receiver at the other end. Bell realized he could transmit a voice in the same way.

Bell knew that Western Union wanted a harmonic telegraph, not a telephone. But he cared deeply about working with the deaf. He knew that speech could be created from electrical vibrations—perhaps a telephone could create speech that the deaf could understand. Bell designed a sound-gathering mouthpiece and ran wires from the attic to a downstairs room. He and Watson talked back and forth. By July they could hear each other, though neither could understand what the other was saying. Bell's lawyer filed a patent on Valentine's Day, 1876—just two hours before Gray filed his patent caveat.

Thomas A. Watson

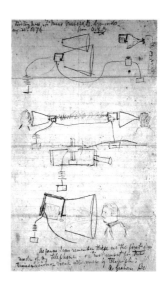

Bell's first sketches of his new invention

Bell's first functional telephone

Legend has it that Alexander Graham Bell spilled acid on himself just as he was about to test his improved telephone, and that's why he called out for Watson as he did. But the story may not be true. No one heard about the acid spill until Watson gave a speech more than thirty years later. Perhaps Watson made up the story to make the moment even more exciting. Or perhaps it did happen, and Bell didn't want anyone to know he'd made a mess!

Checking up on the patent application later, Bell saw Gray's drawing of a liquid transmitter and realized how he could make the sounds clearer. On March 9, Bell tried a liquid transmitter filled with acid. He spoke into the mouthpiece the famous words, "Mr. Watson, come here. I want you!" Watson heard the words clearly and came running.

Who Needs a Telephone?

Bell drummed up interest in his telephone by demonstrating it publicly. He brought it to the Centennial Exposition, which was held in

Philadelphia in 1876 to celebrate the anniversary of the signing of the Declaration of Independence. There, Bell demonstrated the telephone to Dom Pedro, the emperor of Brazil. Dom Pedro dropped the receiver, crying out, "It talks!" He became a staunch supporter of the new telephone. By the end of 1877, Bell had founded the Bell Telephone Company and placed 3,500 telephones in United States homes.

Despite the enthusiasm for Bell's invention, early transmitters didn't work very well. A young inventor named Thomas Edison tried packing grains of carbon into a small container inside the mouthpiece. The carbon intensified the differences in the electrical current created by different sounds, producing a stronger current that could travel farther. Edison's transmitter was eventually combined with Bell's receiver to make a better phone than ever.

Early telephones didn't have bells. The caller had to rap on the mouthpiece loudly until the person at the other end heard. Some callers even used hammers! Thomas Watson invented a bell that solved the problem by letting people know right away that they were being called.

The Centennial Telephone that Bell exhibited in 1876

New York City's switching station in 1896

Early telephones were connected directly to each other by wires—like Hooke's wire system of 1664! A **switchboard** brought the wires of Hartford, Connecticut, to a central location in 1877. At first telephone operators memorized which line belonged to which customer. Callers asked for a person by name, not number. When an 1880 epidemic of measles sent all four operators home sick in Lowell, Massachusetts, Dr. Moses Greeley Parker came up with the idea that each customer should have a number that operators could look up.

Telephones Everywhere!

Telephone lines stretched across America, strung along poles or fence posts. In some rural areas, fence wire was used to carry the telephone signal! Early telephone customers used large, boxy wooden phones that hung on the wall. You spoke into a mouthpiece in the phone box and listened through a bell-shaped receiver on a cord. To place a call, you turned a crank that charged the phone's electromagnet and rang an operator at the switchboard. You then gave the operator the name or number of the person you wanted to call. On the switchboard, every customer's line had an outlet called a jack for incoming calls and a cord with a plug for outgoing calls. The operator would take your cord and stretch it across the switchboard to plug it into the jack for the person you wanted to call.

Almon Strowger, an undertaker in Kansas City, suspected that operators were connecting his calls to competing undertakers. Without an operator, he thought his business would increase. Strowger built the first automatic switching system in 1891. It worked from four buttons on the caller's telephone: one for hundreds, one for tens, one for units, and a reset button.

To call a friend whose number was 859, you would push the hundreds button eight times to send eight pulses to the central switching office. Then you would push the tens button five times and the units button nine times. As you can imagine, people lost count and called a lot of wrong numbers! In 1896 Strowger invented a dial system. Although automatic switching worked well by 1900, many rural communities still used operator-controlled switchboards through the 1930s.

Left: Wall phones like this one were the first at-home telephones.

In rural areas, one wire might serve six or more farms on a party line. While someone at one farm talked on the phone, no one else on the party line could make a call. Anyone who picked up the phone would hear that someone else was talking, then hang up—usually. Sometimes people listened in on each other's conversations—without television, it was the best entertainment around!

Static and poor connections could make calling long distance from home hard on the ears.

Reach Out and Touch Someone

Bell Telephone offered long-distance service, but the longer the distance, the worse the service was. The electrical signal weakened in long wires and sometimes became distorted. Michael Pupin, a Serbian immigrant who had become an electrical engineer in the United States, realized that adding **inductance coils** along the telephone line would keep the signal strong and pure. His "Pupin coils" made long distance possible up to one thousand miles in 1901. But people wanted to talk farther still.

H. E. Shreeve, a Bell engineer, invented a device called a **repeater** that ran the signal through a receiver and another carbon transmitter to renew its strength. Shreeve's system worked, but callers complained of noisy circuits and unclear voices. In 1906 Lee De Forest discovered how to boost an electric current by running it through a tube called an **audion.** Long-distance calls could finally travel as far as telephone lines could reach.

Still, people wanted to place calls where lines didn't go—across the ocean. In 1923 the first New York-to-London call took place, using radio waves to cross the Atlantic Ocean. And in 1945, British scientist and science fiction writer

Arthur C. Clarke suggested that it would be easier to make a long-distance phone call by bouncing a signal off a satellite in outer space. It seemed a fantasy at the time, but this remarkable idea shaped the future of communication.

Alexander Graham Bell makes the first call on a long-distance line from New York to Chicago in 1892.

In the early 1900s at this telephone pay station in Los Angeles, fifty cents could buy a call to San Francisco.

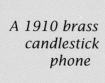

A 1928 desk phone

Phone Fashion

As the phone became an everyday household tool, people looked for ways to turn it into a decoration. The candlestick phones of the early 1900s were a big improvement over the old hand-crank wall telephones. For decades most people opted for a squat, plain black phone that sat on a desk or table. But by the 1960s, people wanted their telephones to blend with their decor. They purchased colored phones or formal, Victorian-style phones with intricately carved bases. Many people opted for fun phones—a tiny, pastel princess phone for a girl's bedroom, or a donut phone whose base and receiver formed a round shape with the dial inside the "donut hole."

A 1910 brass candlestick phone

A 1970s donut phone

This experimental 1952 English phone allowed callers to see each other while they spoke.

More Than Just a Voice

Just as your voice can be transformed into electric current, a picture or a page of words can be, too. In 1914 Edouard Belin connected his invention, the Belinograph, to telephone lines and sent the first news-and-photo fax. In 1956 Bell engineers introduced a telephone that could transmit both the speaker's image and voice. Unfortunately, sending the image was too expensive, and the machine was abandoned.

In the early 1960s, **fiber optics** made it even easier to send messages a long way. Cables made of these glass fibers could carry light across very long distances. Fiber-optic cables could carry more information than radio waves or an old-fashioned telephone wire. When Bell engineers found a way to turn radio waves into light waves, they began using fiber optics to carry telephone calls all over the world.

Fiber-optic cables

Telstar 1 *weighed just 170 pounds, but it changed telephoning forever.*

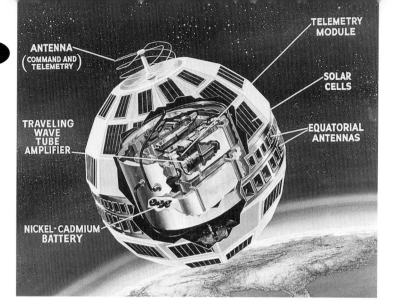

ANTENNA
(COMMAND AND TELEMETRY)

TELEMETRY MODULE

SOLAR CELLS

TRAVELING WAVE TUBE AMPLIFIER

EQUATORIAL ANTENNAS

NICKEL-CADMIUM BATTERY

The second Telstar satellite

In 1962 engineers reflected a laser beam off the moon's surface, proving that signals could be bounced off a satellite—just as Arthur C. Clarke had imagined. On July 10, Bell Laboratories and NASA launched *Telstar 1,* the first telecommunications satellite. A cordless phone has to be within range of a radio tower to send a signal. But a satellite phone can send signals through space to an orbiting satellite, which can transmit them to any telephone anywhere in the world.

Fiber optics and satellite communications don't use analog signals. Your voice still goes into the receiver the same way, but the telephone line that carries it converts the analog signal to a **digital signal.** While an analog signal is a varying electric current, a digital signal is made up of electric impulses that stand for ones and zeros. Digital phone technology can send eight people's voices in the space it would take to send one analog signal!

Computers send and receive information in the form of digital signals, too. When you connect your computer to the Internet over your telephone line, you have to use a modem or a network card to convert your computer's digital signal to an analog signal that can travel across your phone line. As more and more telephone applications require digital technology, phone companies are using new high-speed digital lines that don't carry analog signals at all. Instead, they convert speech directly into a digital signal.

Digital technology has made it possible to send images, as Bell engineers had hoped to do in 1956. You can see who you're talking to if both speakers have a videophone. In some schools, you can even use a videophone to watch your classes if you're home sick. That's a far cry from Philipp Reis listening in on his students! But in spite of the improvements in modern phones, your telephone still uses the same receiver Alexander Graham Bell designed and the same transmitter Thomas Edison invented.

The Internet is a worldwide network of computers that talk to each other through telephone lines. In the 1960s, only a few computers could talk to each other. By the 1990s, kids could chat with other kids, play games, and get help with homework. E-mail lets you zap a message all the way across the world in seconds or minutes. And you can research almost anything on the Internet—even telephones! Check out the Tribute to the Telephone at <http://www.navyrelics.com/tribute/index.htm>.

Instant Communication

Telephones have shrunk the world and speeded it up. You don't have to spend time cooking or driving to a restaurant—you can pick up a phone and order a pizza. Speed dialing even lets you hit one button to call the pizza place instead of punching every digit. And e-mail makes it possible to use one phone call to send a computerized message to every kid on your baseball team, so you don't have to take time to call them individually. People call fast and expect an immediate answer. Even kids carry beepers so they know when their friends (or their parents) are calling.

Imagine living back in the 1800s, when it took weeks for mail to travel across the country. The telegraph could send a message instantaneously, but there were a limited number of wires, and messages stacked up. Family members could talk in person only when they traveled to visit.

With a beeper (above) and an answering machine (opposite page, top), you can be sure you'll know when a friend wants to reach you.

The telegraph and wireless radio made communication easier, but someone had to be listening for the message to get through. When the *Titanic* hit an iceberg in 1912, two-thirds of its passengers and crew died. Many of them might have been saved, but the radio operator on a nearby ship, the *Californian,* was asleep and missed the *Titanic*'s SOS. But a telephone sends a reliable signal that always alerts you when someone is trying to reach you. If you aren't home, the caller can simply leave a message on your answering machine, so you'll get it when you come back.

Some people don't think it's enough to talk on telephones—they want to collect them as well. Many individuals and historical societies collect old wooden box telephones and Strowger switching phones. Classic wall phones can cost four thousand dollars! People who can't get enough of telephones can even subscribe to magazines and newsletters about collecting.

A collectible phone from 1936

The telephone changed lives in another way—by creating a new job opportunity for women. In the early 1900s, few jobs were open to women. Most spent their lives raising families and maintaining their homes, while men earned money. If a woman was unmarried or widowed, however, she had to support herself. The first telephone operators were boys, but they sometimes pulled pranks, such as crossing wires so a caller would end up talking to the wrong person. Telephone companies decided to hire women as operators instead. Emma Nutt of Boston was the first female operator, and by 1946 nearly 250,000 women worked as telephone operators.

A 1915 switchboard operator in Minneapolis

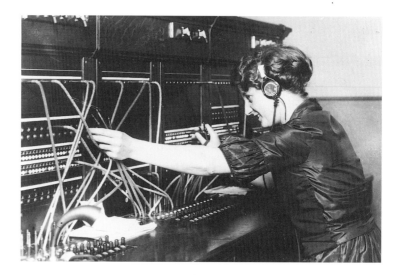

Phone Fun

Perhaps because it talks to us, the telephone has become a star in our culture. Young children have toy telephones with bells that ring and buttons that beep like the real thing. As kids get older, they may use the tones of the telephone's push buttons to play tunes. By the fourth or fifth grade, kids often won't get off the phone at all. They talk to their friends for so long, their parents can't get a call through. In the play and movie *Bye Bye Birdie,* the high school kids tie up all the lines in town gossiping as they sing "The Telephone Hour."

Toy telephones help kids practice dialing—and chatting.

Phones themselves have become an art form. You can buy telephones in the shape of a football or baseball if you're a sports fan. Some phones look like stuffed animals with eyes and mouths that move when the caller talks to you. Or you can get a Snoopy phone, a Mickey Mouse phone, or a Kermit the Frog phone.

R2D2's leg contains the transmitter and receiver in this fun phone.

Making a phone call is often important in television shows, books, and movies. If you want to track down Carmen Sandiego and her evil cohorts, you have to make regular phone calls to the chief and to your contacts. Members of the Baby-Sitters Club set up their jobs by phone. If Miss Piggy doesn't get enough lines in a Muppets special, she just picks up the phone to call her agent. And in the dinosaur movie *Jurassic Park,* the pressure is on computer-savvy Lex Murphy to get the computers up and running so the stranded park visitors can phone for a rescue helicopter before they're eaten by velociraptors.

Movies show the dangers of phones, too. If a telephone rings in a horror movie, it's your cue to scream because there's probably a bad guy on the other end. In *101 Dalmatians,* the villainous Cruella DeVil uses the telephone to find out if the puppies are ready and to call her henchmen to steal them.

A telephone can even be made into art. Salvador Dali created Lobster Telephone *in 1936.*

E.T. makes his first attempt to phone home.

Probably the best example of the enduring nature of the telephone is in the film *E.T.* After the ailing extraterrestrial sees a telephone and a comic strip about sending a signal, he constructs his own version of a telephone to carry his message to his friends in space. When he explains, "E.T. phone home," he gets to the heart of what the telephone gives us: someone who's listening and can help when we need it—someone who's only a phone call away.

Build Your Own Telephone

You will need:

2 styrofoam cups

marker

disposable aluminum pie pan

scissors

butter knife

masking tape

a piece of thin, uncovered wire, such as paddle wire or craft wire*

2 small nuts and bolts

*The wire should be as long as you want your phone to stretch. If you don't have any wire, try string.

When you were little, did you ever make a "telephone" with two cups and a string? String can carry the vibrations created by a voice—but not very far. With a few supplies from around the house, you can build a phone much like the one Robert Hooke invented in 1664.

1. Use the marker to trace the bottom of a styrofoam cup onto the pie pan, two times. Use the scissors to cut out the circles you traced. The circles will be the diaphragms of your telephone.

2. Use the marker to draw a dot in the center of one of the diaphragms. Ask an adult to use the scissors to poke a hole through the dot. The hole should be big enough for the bolt to fit through. Repeat these steps for the other diaphragm.

3. Unscrew the nut from one of the bolts. Wrap one end of the wire three times around the bolt, near the head.

4. Push the bolt through the hole in one of the diaphragms. Screw the nut very tightly onto the bolt. Attach the other end of the wire to the second diaphragm in the same way.

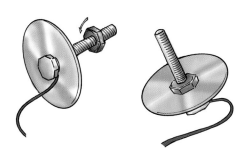

5. Use the butter knife to cut off the bottom of each styrofoam cup. The cups will be the transmitters of your telephone.

6. Tape a diaphragm onto the bottom of each cup so that the nut is on the inside and the wire extends away from the cup. Tape only the edges of the diaphragm. Make sure there are no holes between the diaphragm and the cup.

Ready to Talk?

Ask a friend to hold one cup while you hold the other. Stretch the wire as far and as tight as you can. To speak, cover your entire mouth with the cup and talk loudly. To listen, cover one ear with the cup and use your free hand to hold the other ear closed.

Glossary

analog signal: a varying electric current that transmits sound through a wire

audion: a tube that boosts the strength of an electric current, allowing the current to transmit a voice signal farther

diaphragm: a thin, flexible metal disc in a telephone that moves back and forth in response to sound waves

digital signal: a series of electrical impulses that stand for ones and zeros. The sound of a person's voice can be changed into a digital signal and carried quickly over a telephone line.

electromagnet: a magnet wrapped with wires that carry an electric current. When the electric current is stronger, the magnet's pull gets stronger; when the electric current is weaker, the magnet's pull gets weaker.

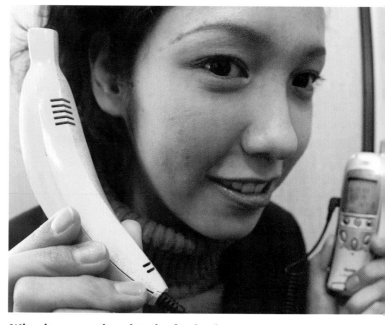

Who knows what kind of telephone inventors will think of next?

fiber optics: thin, clear strands of glass or plastic that transmit a signal in the form of light

harmonic telegraph: a telegraph that can carry different signals on the same wire by sending each signal tuned to a different pitch

inductance coils: coils that can be wrapped around a wire to boost the strength of a signal

multiplex: to carry more than one signal or tone on the same wire

radio waves: electric waves that represent sounds and can travel a long distance through the air

receiver: an earpiece on a telephone. The receiver transforms electric current back to sound so the listener can hear spoken words.

relays: switches that open and close to direct the electric current carrying a telephone call from one wire to another

repeater: a device that can boost the strength of an analog signal. The signal leaves a telephone's transmitter, travels along a wire, and reaches the repeater. The repeater boosts the signal's strength by running it through a receiver and a second transmitter, then sends it along the wire again.

ringback: a ringing sound that a caller hears after dialing a telephone number. The sound lets the caller know that the call is going through to the desired number.

switchboard: a panel used to direct telephone calls. Early switchboards had a plug attached to a wire and an opening called a jack for every telephone owner's line. To connect a call, an operator inserted the caller's plug into the jack for the line the caller wanted to reach.

switching station: in modern telephone systems, a central office where a computer directs each telephone call to the correct line or to another switching station

transmitter: a mouthpiece on a telephone. A transmitter transforms the speaker's voice into electric current.

Index